Advance Praise for *Song for a Single String*

"*Songs for a Single String* is a joyful affirmation of life, but especially of love. Jesús Gardea's poetry awakens a distant, almost forgotten primeval yearning that compels us to find that elusive woman whom we have met only in our dreams, but whose presence we sense will complete us. Always fresh and renewed, he skillfully reaches beyond mere words and brings into focus that elusive feeling we call love."

—Carlos Rubio Albet, author of *The Neophyte: A Dubious Beginning*

"The free verse of Jesús Gardea's *Songs for a Single String* memorializes moments of love discovered, celebrated, lost. Each evokes the quality and forms of *cante hondo,* emphasizing the emotional interplay of human voice and guitar."

—Elizabeth Huergo, Ph.D., writer and English professor

Other Works by Jesús Gardea

Los Viernes de Lautaro
Septiembre y los otros días
El sol que estás mirando
La canción de las mulas muertas
El tornavoz
Soñar la guerra
El alba sombria
Los músicos y el fuego
Sobol
Las luces del mundo
El diablo en el ojo
El agua de las esferas
La ventana hundida
Difícil de atrapar
Juegan los Comensales
Donde el Gimnasta
Reunión de Cuentos
El Biombo y los Frutos

Other Works by Robert L. Giron

Wrestling with Wood
Metamorphosis of the Serpent God
Impressions Françaises
Recuerdos
Songs for the Spirit

CANCIONES PARA UNA SOLA CUERDA

JESÚS GARDEA

SONGS FOR A SINGLE STRING

TRANSLATION BY ROBERT L. GIRON

Gival Press

Arlington, Virginia

CANCIONES PARA UNA SOLA CUERDA.
Copyright © 2002 by The Estate of Jesús Gardea.

Translation: SONGS FOR A SINGLE STRING.
Copyright © 2002 by Robert L. Giron.

All rights reserved under International and Pan-American Copyright Conventions.

Printed in the United States of America.

With the exception of brief quotations in the body of critical articles or reviews, no part of the book may be reproduced or transmitted in any form or by any means, graphic, electronic, or mechanical, including photocopying, recording, taping, or by any information storage or retrieval system, without the permission in writing from the publisher.

Published by Gival Press, an imprint of Gival Press, LLC.
For information please write:
Gival Press, LLC, P. O. Box 3812,
Arlington, Virginia 22203.
Website: givalpress.com

First Edition

ISBN 1-928589-09-X

Library of Congress Card Number 2002108615

Format and design by Ken Schellenberg.

Cover art and illlustrations
"Notes to Myself" © 2000 by Nancy McNamara.

Acknowledgment

Poems 21 and 26 appeared in Spanish with a slightly different English translation in *Puerto del Sol* in the Summer 1982 issue.

*In memory of
Jesús Gardea
whose love poetry
gives me hope.*

— R. L. G.

1

Tú
pan de maravillas
en mi mesa

los árboles
retornan ya

lentamente

al sueño

ven

vamos

que Alguien nos llama

en la tarde

ven.

1

You
bread of marvels
on my table

the trees
return now

slowly

to sleep
come

let's go

Someone calls us

in the evening

come.

2

Voy a buscar para ti
un girasol

un río suave y constante

una plaza
sin vientos

una palabra que triunfe
del cerco

y dos

palomas

para

que

tú

vivas

más alta.

2

I'm going to look for
a sunflower

a river gentle and constant

a plaza
without wind

a word that triumphs
over the wall

and two

doves

so

you

can

live

higher.

3

Yo ardo
como un vaso
hundido en el viento

los tigres

en medio
del humo

celebran mi amor por ti

y tú

nos miras a todos

desnuda

bajo las sombras desnudas de un árbol.

3

I burn
like a glass
buried in the wind

the tigers

in the middle
of the smoke

celebrate my love for you

and you

naked

look at us all

under the naked shadows of a tree.

4

Viento
y dos nosotros

y hojas
que se persiguen
a la luz
de la
luna

y dos

!qué dulce encuentro!

4

Wind
and us two

and leaves
that are followed
in the light
of the moon

and two

What sweet encounter!

5

Una tarde
Tu oro meridional

El aire

El horizonte en mis manos como un barco

Las dulces canciones juntas

y el agua

que me dice

espera
ay! espera.

5

The evening
Your meridional gold

The air

The horizon in my hands like a ship

The sweet songs together

and the water

that tells me

wait
oh! wait.

6

Cuando tú me miras
se despiertan

guitarras
en la boca
del viento

la alegría

y recobro

de pronto

todo lo
perdido

cielos

el fuego

los lirios

y aquellos tigres

que me querían como niños.

6

When you see me

guitars
in the mouth
of the wind
awaken

the joy

and I gather

suddenly

all that

was lost

the skies

the fire

the irises

and those tigers

that loved me like children.

7

Silencio
la clara espiga
está ardiendo

ilumina

hasta el fondo
la cal de mis paredes

me llama
mansamente

Silencio

ella vive
en mí
y quiero oírla.

7

Silence
the clear thorn
is burning

it illuminates

even the bottom
the lime of my walls

it calls me
timidly

Silence

she lives
in me
and I want to hear her.

8

De ti me vienen

como
de un cielo
muy alto

la luz
que abre mis puertas

el aire
inmenso
que impulsa mi barca

los días mejores.

8

From you come

a sky
so high

the light
which open my doors

the air
immense
which propels my boat

the better days.

9

Mira

yo vuelvo a ti
como el río al mar

como la luz y el viento
a las cuerdas
de una guitarra
sola

como
el tigre
al reposo
entre las hierbas

como el sol

como el sol a la tierra.

9

Look

I return to you
like the river to the sea

like the light and the wind
to the strings
of a single
guitar

like
the tiger
to his repose
among the grass

like the sun

like the sun to the earth.

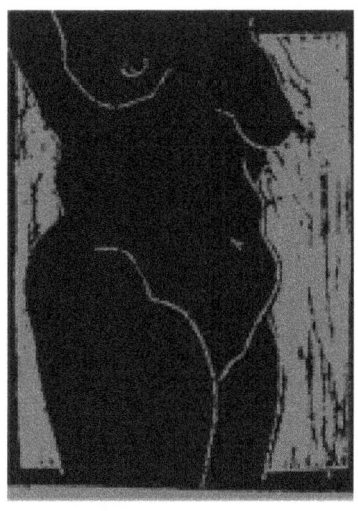

10

Palomas

con el peso
justo de las llamas

de lo callado

una mañana

en mi abierta mano
de hombre
enamorado.

10

Doves

with the just weight
of the flames

of the silenced

a morning

in my open hand
of man
in love.

11

Desde hoy

la vida

transcurrirá
al pie
de aquellos
montes

junto
al trigo

y al servicio del amor que ahí se canta.

11

From this day

life

will transcend
from the foot
of those
mountains

next
to the wheat

and to the service of the love sung there.

12

Te busco
como el viento
a su sombra en los trigales

como el león a la rosa

tiemblas

rodeada
de mí

en mí
ardiendo

luz

del mediodía.

12

I look for you
like the wind
its shadow in the wheat fields

like the lion
the rose

you tremble

surrounded
by me

in me
burning

light

of midday.

13

De ti

no hay nada escrito

tampoco de mí

porque nosotros dos   te digo

vivimos
en el viejo rodar

en el viejo rodar
de las estaciones.

13

Of you

there is nothing written

nor of me

because we two I tell you

live
in the old turn

in the old turn
of the seasons.

14

Tú creces en mí

lluvia
sobre
los montes

creces
hasta
el júbilo

hasta hacerme brotar

en el cuerpo

verdes y claros
resplandores.

14

You grow in me

rain
upon
the mountains

you grow
to
jubilation

until you make me blossom

in the body

green and clear
resplendence.

15

Apenas
te fuiste

salí
a buscarte al viento

entre
los niños

en las últimas
horas
de la tarde

en mí

de noche

como uno que se ha perdido

en ti misma

agua
de todas
mis soledades.

15

You had barely
left

I went
to search for you in the wind

among
the children

in the last
hours
of the afternoon

in me

at night

like one who has lost himself

in you yourself

water
of all
my solitude.

16

Anda
ya la savia
en tu
guitarra

sonando
verde

a sol

a caudalosos tigres

sonando

sonando
en ti
como el viento

como
el dulce
viento
entre
las frutas.

16

Come on
I saw it
in your
guitar

green
sounding

of sun

of abundant tigers

sounding

sounding
in you
like the wind

like
the sweet
wind
among
the fruits.

17

Hondos
árboles
en la
tarde
de tu cuerpo
cuando
escapas
a mi
boca
y a mis
manos de alfarero

llevándote
contigo ay!

llevándote
la luz
y el aire

los ríos
y la gracia
que me hacen falta.

17

Deep
trees
in the
afternoon
of your body
when
you escape
my mouth
and my
potter's hands

carrying
you

carrying
the light
and the air

the rivers
and the grace
that I need.

18

Hay
lirios
que cantan
para ti
en abril

en la
suave tierra
de tus
hombros

en mi boca
nombrada

y en esa luz grande
que nos
alumbra
como un sol
debajo
de otro
sol.

18

There are
irises
that sing
for you
in April

in the smooth
earth of your
shoulders

in my
appointed mouth

and in that grand light
that illuminates us
like a sun
under
another
sun.

19

Idos ya
mis tigres

vuelvo
a tu respiración
de hoja
nueva

a tu presencia de lluvia

de caracol

a mirarte
como te miré
una mañana

allá

al principio
de las
cosas.

19

Gone already
my tigers

I return
to your breath
of new
leaf

to your presence

rain like sea shells

to look at you
as I looked at you
one morning

there

at the beginning
of
things.

20

Ultimo
en tu primavera

yo soy
un hombre
de muy tarde

de lúcidos
tigres
que andan
solos

de canciones
junto
a la oscura
lengua del mundo

pero hombre
que va
a quedar en ti

como
el perfume
de la fruta
en la alta
caja
de las
lluvias.

20

Last
in your spring

I am
a man
too late

of lucid
tigers
that roam
alone

of songs
close by
the dark
tongue of the world

but a man
who will
remain in you

like
the perfume
of the fruit
in the high
box
of the
rainstorms.

21

Me asomé
a mirarte
como el sol
se asoma
a una
casa

dos palomas
tenías
en la sombra

un alhelí
en las blancas
fronteras
de tu
ombligo

agua
de mayo
corriendo
por la
hierbabuena
de tus piernas

me asomé a mirarte

y dos palomas
volaron
hasta
mí.

21

I perched
to look at you
the way the sun
perches upon
a house

you had
two doves
in the shade

a gillyflower
in the white
frontiers
of your
navel

May water
running
along the
mint
of your legs

I perched to see you

and two doves
flew
towards
me.

22

Escúchame en ti:

qué tranquilo

como un profundo río

en mis orillas
están los
tigres

el sueño
de las palomas
que un día
volaron
de mi mano
con la muda
promesa de volver

estoy
yo mismo

y te digo
que lloro
por
las noches

porque
soy muy río

porque

los tigres

porque
las palomas

porque voy tan solo
caminando
rumbo
al mar.

22

Hear me within yourself:

how tranquil

like a deep river

along my shores
are the
tigers

the dream
of the doves
that one day
flew
from my hand
with the mute
promise to return

I am
myself

and I tell you
that I cry
at night

because
I am the river

because
the tigers

because
the doves

because I go so solitary
walking
towards
the sea.

23

Me duele
la primavera

me duele
como una niña
entre los abanicos del mondo

como
una gota reseca
en el paladar

para qué
volvieron
los árboles

quién los llamó

están de más

amor anda solo

tocando
campanas de tierra
al atardecer

y quién
llamó también
a la luz
con todas sus monedas

y a los pájaros

y quién dijo
que este
era el
reino

y que en él nos íbamos
a encontrar
al fin

como el agua
y el fuego

después de los días
del sombrío viento.

23

The spring
hurts me

it hurts me
like a girl
among the fans of the world

like
a dry drop on the palate

why did
the trees
return

who called them

there are too many

love goes about alone

ringing
earthen bells
as evening comes

and who
also called
the light
with all its coins

and the birds

and who said
that this
was the kingdom

and that in it
we would find one another
at the end

like the water
and the fire

after the days
of the somber wind.

24

Dónde
está el trigo

el pan
que íbamos
a cocinar para mañana

no lo sé: aquí
no hay
lugar
para el amor

Vámonos

pues

muriendo
de hambre

de pura pena

como oscuros niños

como semillas
quemadas
por el
viento

vámonos
tornando piedra

sin voz
y sin orejas

y olvidemos ya
que una vez
hablamos
con la rosa

para qué el vino

para qué tanta lluvia acariciando el aire

para qué habitar
casas de madera clara
si luego tenemos
que abandonarlas al polvo

dónde está el trigo

dónde

dónde está el pan.

24

Where
is the wheat

the bread
we were
going to bake for tomorrow

I don't know: here
there is no
room
for love

Let's go

then

dying
of hunger

of pure shame

like dark children

like seeds
burnt
by the
wind

let's go
turning rocks

voiceless
and earless

and let us forget now
that once
we spoke
with the rose

why the wine

why so much rain caressing the air

why inhabit
houses of clear wood
if later we have
to abandon them to the dust

where is the wheat

where

where is the bread.

25

No quiero
entrar
solo
por las
puertas
del agua
este verano

contigo
quiero entrar

secretamente
y cantando

contigo

contigo

por las puertas
del agua
este verano.

25

I don't want
to enter
alone
through the
doors
of the water
this summer

with you
I want to enter

secretly
and singing

with you

with you

through the doors
of the water
this summer.

26

Un día
voy a encontrarte

para siempre

en el agua
que bebo

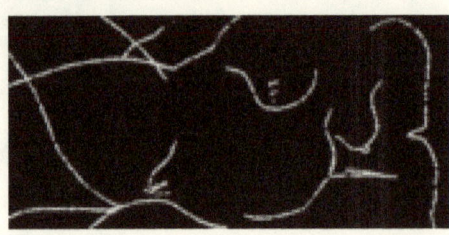

por
camino
de altas
hierbas

de soles
claros

cantando tú

mirándote yo como acostumbro

como a una
flor

como
a una ventana
de luz
abierta
en mis
manos.

26

One day
I'm going to find you

for ever

in the water
I drink

along
the path
of high
grass

of clear
suns

you signing

me looking at you like I'm accustomed

as if at a
flower

as if
at a window
of light
open
in my
hands.

Books Available from Gival Press

Barnyard Buddies I by Pamela Brown; illustrations by Annie H. Hutchins
 1st edition, ISBN 1-928589-15-4, $16.00

> Thirteen stories filled with a cast of creative creatures both engaging and educational. "These stories in this series are delightful. They are wise little fables, and I found them fabulous." — Robert Morgan, author of *This Rock* and *GapCreek*

Bones Washed With Wine: Flint Shards from Sussex and Bliss by Jeff Mann
 1st edition, ISBN 1-928589-14-6, $15.00

> A special collection of lyric intensity, including the 1999 Gival Press Poetry Award winning collection. Jeff Mann is "a poet to treasure both for the wealth of his language and the generosity of his spirit." — Edward Falco, author of *Acid*

Canciones para sola cuerda — Songs for a Single String by Jesús Gardea
 English translation by Robert L. Giron 1st edition, ISBN 1-928589-09-X, $15.00

> A moving collection of love poems, with echoes of Neruda à la Mexicana. "Jesús Gardea's poetry awakens a distant, almost forgotten primeval yearning that compels us to find that elusive woman whom we have met only in our dreams, but whose presence we sense will complete us."
> — Carlos Rubio Albet, author of *The Neophyte: A Dubious Beginning*

Dervish by Gerard Wozek
 1st edition, ISBN 1-928589-11-1, $15.00

> *Winner of the 2000 Gival Press Poetry Award.* This rich whirl of the dervish traverses a grand expanse from bars to crazy dreams to fruition of desire. "By Jove, these poems shimmer." — Gerry Gomez Pearlberg, author of *Mr. Bluebird*

Dreams and Other Ailments — Sueños y otros achaques by Teresa Bevin
 1st edition, ISBN 1-928589-13-8, $21.00

> *Winner of the Bronze Award - 2001 ForeWord Magazine's Book of the Year Award for Translation.* A wonderful array of short stories about the fantasy of life and tragedy but filled with humor and hope. "*Dreams and Other Ailments* will lift your spirits." — Dr. Lynne Greeley, Professor of Theatre, University of Vermont

The Gay Herman Melville Reader by Ken Schellenberg
    1st edition, ISBN 1-928589-19-7, $16.00

    A superb selection of Melville's work. "Here in one anthology are the selections from which a serious argument can be made by both readers and scholars that a subtext exists that can be seen as homoerotic." — David Garrett Izzo, author of *Christopher Isherwood: His Era, His Gang, and the Legacy of the Truly Strong Man*

Let Orpheus Take Your Hand by George Klawitter
    1st edition, ISBN 1-928589-16-2, $15.00

    Winner of the 2001 Gival Press Poetry Award. A thought provoking work that mixes the spiritual with stealthy desire, with Orpheus leading us out of the pit. "These poems present deliciously sly metaphors of the erotic life that keep one reading on, and chuckling with pleasure." — Edward Field, author of *Stand Up, Friend, With Me*

Metamorphosis of the Serpent God by Robert L. Giron
    1st ed., ISBN 1-928589-07-3, $12.00

    "Robert Giron's biographical poetry embraces the past and the present, ethnic and sexual identity, themes both mythical and personal."
    — The Midwest Book Review

The Nature Sonnets by Jill Williams
    1st edition, ISBN 1-928589-10-3, $8.95

    An innovative collection of sonnets that speaks to the cycle of nature and life, crafted with wit and clarity. "Refreshing and pleasing."
    — Miles David Moore, author of *The Bears of Paris*

Songs for the Spirit by Robert L. Giron
    1st ed., ISBN 1-928589-08-1, $16.95

    This humanist psalter reflects a vision of the new millennium, one that speaks to readers regardless of their religion. "This is an extraordinary book." — John Shelby Spong, author of *Why Christianity Must Change or Die: A Bishop Speaks to Believers in Exile*

Wrestling with Wood by Robert L. Giron
    3rd ed., ISBN 1-928589-05-7, $5.95

    A chapbook of impressionist moods and feelings of a long-term relationship which ended in a tragic death. "Nuggets of truth and beauty sprout within our souls." — Teresa Bevin, author of *Havana Split*

For Book Orders Only, Call: 800.247.6553
Or Write : Gival Press, LLC / PO Box 3812 / Arlington, VA 22203
Or Visit: www.givalpress.com

www.ingramcontent.com/pod-product-compliance
Lightning Source LLC
Chambersburg PA
CBHW031214090426
42736CB00009B/915